Robot Fun and Games

by Sydnie Meltzer Kleinhenz
illustrated by Rich Stromoski

Orlando   Boston   Dallas   Chicago   San Diego

Visit *The Learning Site!*
www.harcourtschool.com

Robot Riddles

When a robot decides to clean its parts, what does it use? *Bath oil!*

What does a robot say when
its cells go bad and it buys a
new battery?
Charge it!

3

What trick does the circus
robot do?
It flips its switch!

What did the rolling robot say
to the dancing robot?
I'm the wheel thing!

Make a Robot

1. Cut a circle in the middle of the bottom of a paper bag.
2. Cut a circle in each side for your arms.

3. Have a grown-up slice the ends off of four empty cereal boxes to fit your arms and legs.

4. Cut slits and circles in cereal boxes for your feet.
5. Have a grown-up cut off the handle side and the top of a plastic jug.

6. Put the bag on your body
   and slide the boxes in place.
7. Place the jug on your head
   so your face shows.

Practice robot-talk. Almost
always keep your voice even.
Make each sentence sound
choppy.

10

Once you look and sound like a robot, pretty soon you'll start thinking like a robot.

Remember, robots can't
think for themselves!

Race a Robot

Two "robots" start in the same place. They decide on a finish line. A third player rolls the number cubes with two hands.

The right-hand roll shows the steps the robot on the right takes. The left-hand roll shows the steps the robot on the left takes.

Robots always race on stiff legs.

The robot who wins the race
rolls the number cube.
Try it again!